Transformational Journey

– PAUL ERRANDS –

An environmentally friendly book printed and bound in England by
www.printondemand-worldwide.com

This book is made entirely of chain-of-custody materials

www.fast-print.net/store.php

Transformational Journey

ISBN 978-178035-282-4

First published 2012 by
FASTPRINT PUBLISHING
Peterborough, England.

Transformational Journey by Paul Errands

Contents

Learning to know and LOVE YOURSELF

About the author and book

Well done! This is a BRILLIANT and helpful source of information to have. My name is Paul Errands, and I am currently 17 years young. I found true self love and the ability to understand myself in late 2011. This knowledge has grown with me all the way and it is a successful skill to have. And best of all, it's something I want to share with you all.

I have written this book for children, teenagers and adults to read and discover that there is a reason to be living a life surrounded around self-love and respect. Right from a young age I had the ability to stand up for what I believed in however certain situations overtook the power of that such as bullying and weight issues.

I want people to know that it's ok to be different and to have such uniqueness (es) within this world. The earlier you can learn to love yourself; I believe the longer and more successful life you lead. And why not- You deserve it.

This book can be read individually or out to a group. Either way I believe my message that every individual in this world is special and are to be proud to be who or what they are. No matter what sex you are, whether you are black or white, no matter is you are gay, straight or both, no matter if you come from a broken home or if you have disabilities. The key is to love you regardless.

Every situation we are in influences our lives and can be viewed as some of the more powerful gifts of life the world has given us. The fact I went through a phase of "I hate myself" meant I had something to overcome and sort out.

I know now that I wasn't alone and there were ways around these situations. I just had to find them and this book is out here to show people that you don't have to wait till your half way through your life to find out that you are special and deserve the very best in life.

Tragedies only happen for a reason! You are still living your life. Do not see your life as a survival stage. Live your life and in the world of "HAPPINESS AND SUCCESS".

START YOUR SUCCESS **NOW!!**

Definition of Self Love: *"The ability to respect yourself and feel from within you are actually worth respect and the very best in the world. Through having self-love, you become more connected and confident to yourself and others around you. Self-love and respect is **not** selfishness- It's showing that **YOU ARE WORTH SOMETHING**!! It comes from within and you feel **PROUD** to be **YOU!**"*

My personal definition:

Successful

Energised

Luxury

Feeling **F**ABULOUS

Living

Opportunities

Valued

Exciting

Definition of true Happiness: *"Feeling the butterflies of **excitement** for the simplest things such as doing your hair, brushing your teeth, creating a positive and meaningful smile, writing a book, watching a video or a film. Finding true HAPPINESS was one of the* *best **FREE SKILLS** for me to find. And yes there are people with millions of pounds out there, yes there are people who are out there famous etc. But the true happiness comes from feeling **HAPPY** and **EXCITED** from within."*

I have been through a lot within my 17 years of life however I don't fall into the "poor me" zone because I don't believe in dwelling in negativity. I have been told that with what I have been through in life, people don't know how I can be so happy and positive about my life. I have been told that I am "The happiest person they know"- That made me feel it's obviously showing that I have a lot of respect for myself and its actually meaning something.

The saying "Actions speak louder than words" has obviously been met here because it's not just words, I am generally happy with life, I really do LOVE MYSELF, I don't dwell on the bad times from the past and best of all, people are actually noticing my true happiness.

The key is to relive the bad times, but not fall into the situations again. I spend time alone or with others healing bad times that has happened in my life. However, the emotions will come up when they're ready to. Things only happen for a reason.

I believe that this book will come into good use, and I look forward to hearing your responses to this healing and valued source of information. This book isn't just aimed at people my age, but it is available to help everyone, including groups of people such as families and groups of friends.

Best Regards

Paul Errands x

I believe you can do it. I did it and I'm showing everyone else out there that they can do the same.

Chapter 1: The beginning

At this moment in time, you are probably thinking well where do I start and how do I do it? It's simple. Follow this book and the different methods of connecting to yourself to discover that what you want is actually out there. You just have to find it. I know because I have the knowledge and the experience in this feature from such a young age, and I am willing to share with you my experiences and how I turned the situations back round to into a positive. The way I work is turning a negative into a positive.

OK, let's start from the very beginning. The fact that you have even picked this book up means you are a step closer to loving yourself and getting connected to yourself once again. The starting point is acceptance (this is where I started).

There is no point in fighting for something that you aren't or what you don't have. You are to accept that you have been given by god and the universe this life, this body, this family, this house you live in as well as this opportunity to connect to your inner-self once again.

There is no point in saying "I wish I was......" because it isn't going to happen. You have been given this life for a reason. Everything happens for a reason. What happens to you is meant to happen. What doesn't happen wasn't supposed to happen. Life is a flow of energy and the key is to flow with the energy rather than against it.

You probably have picked this book up because you want to know how to view the world on a more positive level, become more in tune with yourself and to find the ability to view a positive side within yourself rather than a negative; you have already made a stepping stone through purchasing this unique and helpful source of information. To start, I will share with you the powerful starting tool, which I started off with, is accepting who you really are.

The way I was when I hit rock bottom was yes I was fat, I was insecure, I was emotional and most of all out of control (eating wise especially). I had no self-confidence at this point. I had learnt the skills of what I needed to do to lose weight but the fact was, I didn't want to even put the effort into loving myself. It wasn't until I actually finished going to the local bakery for two sausage rolls and a chocolate chip cookie, 1 ½ litre bottle of coke, huge packet of cheese flavoured Doritos and a caramel KITKAT from the local super market just across from where I lived one night that I knew this wasn't the way forward. Baring in mind I had this sort of food for almost 17 years.

Having lost weight previously but gained it again through the lack of self-esteem, love and respect, I had put it back on with even more weight. I went from being 7 ¾ stone (when I was 15) to being 10 ½ stone (at the age of 16) within a year of indeed a lot of changes. These included moving house, losing friends and family members.

Breathing in every time I looked in the mirror to make myself satisfactory with the way I looked was the only way I managed to convince myself I could have another sharing bag of crisps, another chocolate bar, two sausage rolls and a cookie all to myself; only to really see I was fooling myself.

I finally admitted defeat one day when I looked into the mirror and burst into tears. I had hit rock bottom. BUT! I said to myself- "OK- I've hit rock bottom now. I've been bullied for the way I look, I've abused myself and now's the time to change it all". And the power came from that minute I stood up and looked at how I looked and I said "I'm sorry Paul, it won't happen ever again!"

Now that was when I was fat, emotional, insecure etc. because I had about 4 people who were there for me. I tried fighting it for a very long time but sadly I didn't seem to win. It was either to stay as I was or to change. I decided to change for the better. Having accepted that I was fat, I was insecure, I was emotional etc. I was then able to put a plan into place to correct these "faulty features". Accepting this was the key to moving forward.

The key to accepting yourself is one of the most painful things you ever have to do because it's about being 101% honest with yourself. If you can do that- you are 1/5 of the way there already. I wrote down everything I was feeling at the time with the solutions next to it and I had about 3 sides of A4 on faults. Sadly I found it hard to find a solution to the problems. Being a spiritualist and having the ability to ask my "source" what I am to do, they gave me the answers. They showed me that id hit rock bottom and the only way was UP! This was an incentive in itself and I managed to receive the correct solutions to the issues I had found with myself. They showed me a detox plan that I was to use to lose weight and the foods I was to eat- and I decided to stick to it.

Definition of Acceptance: *"Being 101% truthful to yourself and not hiding from what you feel about yourself! Finding at a deep level your true feelings on what you feel and what you believe you deserve and why? Finding a solution to every problem is also key because there is a solution to every problem."*

Acceptance task: This does help finding your true feelings about yourself. Copy down the table below and write your true feelings about yourself and in the solution column, write down what you want to do about these feelings. Make sure the solutions are going to be 1) Achievable and 2) Realistic. Don't put something down that you are not prepared to stick to.

How do I feel about myself? What am I?	**Solutions to my feelings. Remember: What you feel may not be true.**
Eg) I feel I am worthless because I look ugly	*Change my thought patterns. I feel like this because............ I am not ugly- it's just a feeling. Really I am beautiful.*
Eg) I am fat because people bully me.	*Prove I can lose weight Eg) Diet etc.*

Continue with your own version of this and draw how you see yourself now and how you would like to see yourself in the future. List all issues you find with yourself but make sure you find a solution to all the problems. It doesn't matter if you end up with hundreds of faults because you will also have hundreds of solutions too at the end of it.

Chapter 2: Treating yourself

Well Done. You now know that it's important to accept who you are however it is equally important to rewards yourself for taking a huge step in your transformational journey. Choose something you really like so if its watching a film go and watch a film, if you like shopping go shopping. Treat yourself when you do something positive towards you and your future.

Unlike an exam where you have to do what's on the paper, and the rewards are a grade, this is actually about you. You set the tasks and you set the rewards. However don't be too easy or too hard with the rewards. I'm not saying reward yourself too little but make the rewards realistic to the tasks you have completed.

"I allow myself regular rewards. I am a strong person from within to my outer body. I deserve to become a success"

Because one of my solutions to my weight issue was to lose weight, I never treated myself with food. I treated myself with things I enjoyed doing. Whether that would be going on a bus journey to somewhere new or buying myself some new clothes, I always found an alternative to food. Food would have put a hold on my weight loss and the fact I even said NO to food meant I found one of the most powerful tools I have ever come across. Inner strength and willpower.

I even made my own certificates and stars saying "Well done! You are a star!" Small little gifts like this builds such a strong bond and connection with yourself. I realised then- my true path of success was being created in front of my eyes. The power was just beginning.

Even spending time alone was an incentive to me. Doing whatever I liked to do in my spare time such as search the internet, watching videos, playing games etc. That was an incentive and I love spending time with friends however I also enjoy spending time alone to work on myself that little bit further.

Chapter 3: Finding your inner self

Through actually putting the solutions to the problems into place and rewarding myself for staying on task, the next stage was to build a connection with myself.

The affirmation I said to myself every day was:

"I deserve to be Number 1. I am number 1 in my life" because I wanted to develop myself further. At first when I said this it didn't mean anything. But you have to keep going and believing in it. Eventually you find yourself finding the seep of belief within yourself and that's it- it can only grow bigger. When I actually believed I was worth something, it was coming through- breaking through in fact.

The key was to never ever give up on the feeling that you are actually worth something. It may take hours, days or even weeks but if you keep with it and tell yourself you are doing this for YOU and YOU ONLY- I promise you it comes eventually. And it's the best feeling ever.

Remember everything happens for a reason. If you find yourself not believing in the affirmation then you need to review your whole life in general. Are you being negative elsewhere in your life? These blockages are preventing you from living the life of your dreams. It is possible to live your dream life even if you are at rock bottom but only if you put the hard work into it. I never said this was going to be easy but it's easier than going through life feeling poor about yourself. Everybody likes to feel good about what they do so why wouldn't anyone want to work on themselves? Only you can decide for you.

When I was connecting to spirit one night, my mind showed me as a new person (thin, good looking, proud to be me) give me as I was at the time (developing through a detox programme) a big hug within that hug was positive energy and belief. Wisdom came to me and said" I can do this. You are doing so well. Don't give up now. You are making progress- keep it up".

For Christmas the year before I was given this blue monkey which was called "Little Paul" which was to be used whenever I felt hurt or upset as something I could give a hug. It represented my inner child. Up until this point I had no self of steam so I always thought oh what is the point in using it? But this connection brought this blue monkey and the newer me gave me the blue monkey to hug. The message was to use this monkey as a relief strategy of whenever I was upset and wanted a hug myself, all I had to do was actually give it a hug.

"I am allowed to work on myself. Those who say I'm not are only jealous of my development in life. I believe and know I am worth something to me. I love myself dearly"

The fact I had something visible in front of me to actually hold and cuddle that actually symbolised me meant I could work better with myself and my inner child at the same time. The fact Little Paul symbolised my inner child meant I felt better inside and also showed me that I am looking after myself and becoming more connected with myself. It gave me something to look at and love physically but at the same time love my real inner child. The way I knew it was working was through the emotions that were coming up and the amount of crying I did. I knew then it was ok to cry. Having people around me who said it was ok to cry helped too.

The key that helped me was that I had a physical object to work on. Find or buy a physical object such as a soft toy to represent you. Feel as if you are working with someone else however that someone else is really you. It isn't babyish; never ever believe you are childish because you play with a soft toy because you're not. All it's about is working on yourself because you want to. You want to show yourself some affection. Who wouldn't really if they had come this far? Only those who daren't come this far and who are too negative will say no to that question. Eventually you will find yourself being able to hug yourself but it will take time.

Hugging yourself is something I do every single night before I go to sleep. From when I got to this stage of the self-development process, I felt the touch of myself with the healing power that somebody else could have given to me. I find it loving and warming that I have found that I can hug myself and allow it to mean so much to me. It makes me feel really connected to whom I really am and I feel that I can cope with any situation when I hug myself.

Eg: Like a little child who has hurt themselves through falling over or hitting their head on a table, they go to the parents for caring gestures. I feel when I feel hurt and I need a hug, I can actually receive that hug by myself and give body the respect that I really do deserve.

Chapter 4: It's ok to cry

Being a boy, a lot of people said it was wrong for a boy to cry. A boy if he has feelings should forget about them- its only girls that cry. That is in fact **wrong**!!! Boys have feelings too which cannot be avoided. Pushing down the feelings meant I was only going to have to resurface them again. There is no way that anybody doesn't have feelings. Everybody from young to old will have emotional feelings about or towards someone, something, a place or even themselves.

To push down feelings, you can use food, drink, drugs, cigarettes etc. I had done that with food and drink before and I wasn't prepared to do it again. As I went along further on my journey- I found myself becoming stronger with my mind. I actually found it within to easily say NO to the bad and YES to the good. I remember the first time I did this and I cried of happiness. I was officially on the journey of **"self-development"**. To say how easy it is to say yes to fall back into old habits, the feeling that I said no meant I had **SELF CONTROL!** This is something that means so much to me.

Whenever you are feeling bad, upset, down or you just want to cry- do it. Cry your heart and emotions out. It's better than sabotaging all your hard work by pushing them down. Crying isn't a girl thing. Boys can cry whenever they want about anything they want too. It's a human right at the end of the day. The fact that people say that when you cry you are pathetic etc. means that they daren't cry. They daren't open up to who they really are. Trust that you can always be yourself and work on **YOU** whenever you want to. You are allowed to heal your hurts.

You don't have to cry in front of people if you don't want to. You can go into a room alone and cry for however long you like. Crying is natural- all babies cry and they aren't afraid to show it. Crying is just another releasing strategy that the body knows what to do. One of the best I would say.

"Crying is amazing when you know you're letting the paid, the emotion and the feeling out"

Crying can occur for two reasons. Crying of happiness and crying of sadness. Both of which I have done and probably what everyone has done within their lifetimes. Both are good reasons to cry. Don't ever be afraid to let out your true colours or what you are really feeling. Letting them up and out to the surface is just another opportunity for you to make more of a success in the world. It's something you can deal with there and then rather than pushing more food, drink, drugs, alcohol etc. into your body.

Definition of crying: *"Crying is an escape route for emotions. Crying releases emotions and allows you to feel better from within the body to the outside. Crying is natural and is ok to cry. It is one of the simplest ways to express how you feel to yourself and shows that you are working with your feelings truthfully."*

"I am allowed to cry and show my true feelings. My feelings are worthy and are to be listened to and most importantly acknowledged by myself"

Remember to talk to people if you can on how you feel but most of all, be honest with yourself about your feelings. Talk to someone you trust however always know you can trust yourself no matter what. You are not alone. Someone is willing to listen even if it is **YOU!**

"I AM WORKING WITH MY FEELINGS TRUTHFULLY AND HONESTLY! I AM STRONG!"

Chapter 5: It's OK to be different- Having self-confidence and respect from within

When you are now working with yourself on a deep level- you are over half way there with the personal development process. When I was doing all this work for myself (all the accepting, the regular treating myself, the powerful work with my inner child and allowing myself to cry), I felt like my life was inside a tunnel. A tunnel in which I had become trapped within for almost 16 years.

However, now the light at the end of the tunnel was in my site, a positive feeling of self-praise, self-confidence and self-respect had emerged out of nowhere. It was again another incentive I found inside me and was part of my personal-development journey. I had reached the point of no return now.

And then the comments started. "What a weirdo", "who on earth would want to love themselves". My answer was "ME! I deserve to be loved by me. I deserve more than what I've had."

Discovering the self-belief I had meant I was viewed by others as different. Different in my eyes doesn't mean bad. I don't believe in the bad or negative approach anymore. I believe I had created my unique spot in life where I could be the true me rather than a sheep that follows the crowds.
I always said that sheep are not my type of animal. Sheep may be nice and fluffy on the outside but it's what's on the inside that counts. If you are to go through life following the crowds by having the latest phone, the latest clothes or gadgets, you need to ask yourself "Does this make me HAPPY?" and "What does HAPPY mean to me?"

For myself, I get a lot of people saying "you are always happy and positive" because they see I am a smiling and fully energised person from the core of who I really am.

However, the happiness to these people may differ to my personal definition of the word "HAPPY".

Definition of HAPPY: *"with the power of within and the EXCITEMENT bouncing around over the simplest of situations"*

Happiness is shown on two levels; the inner level and the outer level. Both levels of happiness need to be met in order for someone to be truly happy. The inner level of happiness is the one inside of you, the one you feel inside. The outer level is the one that SHOWS the happiness of someone.

A meaningful smile is rooted from within the core of who you really are. As much as it is said that everybody is different, many believe they are the same as someone else. They key is to see that you are different, your smile, your definitions and interpretations of words, colours etc. are indeed different.

Be proud to have a unique spot within this world. Your happiness comes from the within. Your insides and core of who you are differs to everybody else's meaning that your happiness is different to everybody else's.

Don't be afraid to show your differences.

"I AM PROUD TO BE DIFFERENT. I AM ENTITLED TO MY OWN OPPINIONS, DEFINITIONS AND INTERPRETATIONS OF EACH AND EVERY SITUATION I FIND MY LIFE COPING SUCCESSFULLY WITHIN. I

AM MY OWN INDIVIDUAL AND THIS IS MY LIFE. MY LIFE IS COMPLETE WITH WHAT I HAVE AND WHAT I HAVE IS HAPPY WITH ME."

When I wake up each and every morning, I take a good look in the mirror and say "Paul, YOU ARE AMAZING & UNIQUE" meaning I start my day of positively rather than negatively. Because today is the day you are living and how you start your day is how your day is going to continue.

Every morning when I shower, I see it as a loving respectful gift to myself to keep clean, healthy and smelling nice. I like to keep clean as a matter of respect towards myself, my body and my soul. Brushing my teeth I always see as a respectful treatment towards myself.

Respect towards you is a key element of balanced goodness to yourself. When you cleanse yourself (internally or externally), you are giving your life respect, when wearing nice smart clothes, again you are giving yourself respect. As I personally become more respectful towards myself, I always want to look unique as my own person (different from everyone else), feel inside I am worth positive success that brings joy to the day of which I am living.

"I am respectful towards myself. My amounts of self-respect increase with the joys of which today brings"

When you respect someone or something, there is an element of love and passion towards that certain someone or something. Respect is found easier to give to others rather than ourselves and this is something which needs to stop because when you respect yourself, you are not dependent upon anybody else giving you it. Giving yourself the attention you need means you are in control of your life and your feelings.

This is YOU who I am talking about. Not the neighbour down the road, not the local shop keeper or the man who walks the dog every morning past your house, I'm talking about YOU and taking in the respect that you deserve from within yourself, I can assure that you as a whole become an independent source of LIFE within the world we live in. And to be honest, who wouldn't want to really?

Chapter 6- Meaningful Mirror Work

It took me a long time to be able to look in the mirror and see beauty in me. When I was eating the foods on which made me feel happy temporarily, I couldn't look in the mirror. I was always thinking "oh gosh there's another mirror, look away!"

Now I'm constantly being told by people to stop "checking myself out" in the mirror- which I find quite funny really. Rather than me saying I can't believe the remarkable difference, I am going to say I can believe it because I was the one who went through it.

The difference between when I was big and to the point I am at now is absolutely mind pleasing. It makes me so proud of what I have done and from such as young age, I am always told I have huge amounts of inner strength and willpower to say no to these foods and actually want to develop further on in life.

Definition of inner strength: *"Finding it within to give your body what it needs and not to give in to what it doesn't need. Inner strength relates to the strength inside of us. It has a very positive effect on our minds and our mind set on the ways we do things and act in certain situations. It is easily accessed only if you want it to work and want to find it especially on a transformational journey of life."*

Every morning, I look in the mirror and smile from out to within. I am now not afraid to look into the mirror and I have a deep conversation with myself. It's a powerful gift that I have. I love to find out how I feel from within. I look deep into my eyes and say "I LOVE ME". Just little comments like this starts my day on a positive note however the key is to believe in what you are saying about yourself. I do believe I am an amazing and wonderful person. I know I am no worse or no better than anybody else in this world. I am unique and amazing at what I do best. You are too. You should be pleased to see uniqueness(es) inside of you.

"I am my own unique person. Everything I do today marks a meaningful situation of my life. What I see staring back at me in the mirror is someone I adore. I LOVE BEING ME!"

Mirror work is all about looking in the mirror and building up a positive connection with yourself. The sooner you start to believe in yourself and know you are worth something, your life is always in the fast lane heading towards the sky.

Look what's up above us; the universe which has no ending and that's where your life is heading. UP, UP AND UP! Free to be who and what it really is.

Chapter 7- Going for the BEST! Being the BEST!

One successful strategy that I learnt through self-love and respect was a new way of coping with bullying. When I got called "Gay pr**k", "loner boy", "fatty fatty bum bum" etc., the best way was to not allow it in. It's easy really. Trust me.

One day I was at my school sat in the canteen eating a banana and a cheese roll and I got rubbish thrown at me because the teachers were not around to stop them. The rubbish hit me on the head and I looked around and said "Who threw that". The lad in the corner of the canteen said "Me ya fatty gay boy!"

Now, at one point I would have said "F**k off t*at" but do you know what I did? I agreed with them. I said "Yes you are right! I am fat and I am gay. Have you got a problem with that?" Obviously I didn't believe it. I felt good about being me and on a diet. It made me even determined to lose more weight.

Now the fact that I agreed with the bully, the conversation was ended from that point because they hadn't got anything to go on. After that I realised that it was what I thought and felt inside that counted not the bully's words and thoughts. And that is one way of building up your confidence by agreeing with what anybody is saying about you but not caring that they think badly of you. Because it's what you think of you that means something.

However, I now only allow positive comments to come to me because I know that I am not fat anymore, I know that I am not gay. But so what if I was gay. It's nothing bad, it is part of nature. I don't have anything against them because they're no different to anybody else.

That is something else I want others to know that if you are thinking about being gay or something you don't feel comfortable in admitting to others, I can assure you that there is nothing wrong with you. It's part of you. Don't be ashamed of it.

Don't ever be afraid to say you are worth something. It's the way you live your life that counts. Not how someone else does. Remember your life is all about you.

Listen to what your body is saying to you. When you do feel you want to ask your body a question- DO IT!

Close your eyes and ask your body what you want to ask it. Your body will tell you either through a feeling, emotion, sound or touch.

Don't ever forget that you are NUMBER 1 in your life. Don't believe that anyone is better or brighter than you because in life, we all have strong and weak elements. Everyone is unique and has equal amounts of strong and weak points.

The fact that I have accepted myself, developed upon myself and my thoughts, feelings and emotions, understand that I am worth something and that I am an amazing person in this world, the negatives that were once there are now healed with positives.

"I am the way I am for a reason and I love being me"

Chapter 8- Forgiveness isn't easy

As you have probably realised now, that school life during late 2010 and early 2011 hadn't been the easiest of times for myself however I know it could have been a lot worse.

However I now know that life has given me the "opportunity" (as I like to call it) to be bullied and I am thankful that life actually did do such a thing because it has made me a stronger person within and made me see life in a completely different angle which made my start to 2012 a very special one.

It wasn't until I finished school that I was thinking about the bad times of what I saw of school life and I said "thank you" out of nowhere. It then became clear I was thanking the universe for the experience of being bullied because I am one person who is proud to be different- otherwise I would have followed the crowds. I don't mind now being looked at by people and those thinking gosh he's weird or he's not normal because I always say "what is normal?" and people can't answer that question because everybody is different. Different doesn't mean bad. Don't ever believe being different is something bad because it isn't.

Don't forget, I was at this powerful point of nearly finishing my 3 month weight loss program when I said thank you to the universe.

That day, I continued to think to myself of all the bullies and all of what they had done to me that I said with open arms ***"I forgive you. I know you have made mistakes in life, so have I but I forgive you".***

At this point all I felt like doing was crying. Not crying because I was upset about what the bullies had done, oh no, I was crying because of happiness. I felt and still do to this day that I have reached a huge stepping stone across the flowing river of life. I know that the forgiving part did take a while and I will admit it was hard to do so. But eventually it naturally came and I forgive every person in this world who has made mistakes because I am a forgiving person.

Obviously I won't forget what happened because at the end of the day, it was a lifelong lesson that I needed to learn. And that was to cope with bullying and start looking after number one.
Number one being ME!

My advice to you would be to naturally spend 1 hour now and think of the people who you know have made mistakes concerning you. Just think about what they have done for one hour and when you're ready, speak with the universe:

"Thank you "NAME", you have taught me a life lesson. What you did wasn't nice and I won't forget it. However I forgive you as you made a mistake like everyone else does in the world."

And then put the situation at peace. You may feel that there's some stored anger towards these people and I advise to see a healer in getting these emotions out to the open.

I see myself as my own healer in life through having the ability to use techniques such as EFT (emotional freedom techniques) where you take on certain pressure points to overcome situations and connecting with spirit through asking spirit questions of what I should and shouldn't be doing. Even blowing the pains out either into the atmosphere or into a balloon helps me to do such powerful relief.

Powerful techniques such as these help me through healing situations and I am sure I will be doing them at some point soon as I know I still need to heal more. However seeing life in a different angle, I can now say that I have a head start in life through being able to speak my feelings out, heal them and make them into a positive affirmation.

"I trust life that I have been given these techniques to help myself and others around the world. I am different and proud to be of my own uniqueness. I am deeply loved by myself and others and I am thankful that I am loved and appreciative for what I have in life"

Chapter 9- Laughing

This chapter will be very short. I laugh for at least a good 10 minutes every day at least whether it's with friends or on my own. I always enjoy a good laugh.

Laughing symbolises fun to me and I want to live a life where fun is around me. It is now a reality to have fun around me every day and every night.

Laughing has brought positivity and fun into my life and in 2012 I have every single day woken up with a huge smile upon my face which shines all day, every day.

I like to start my day of on a positive note and every morning I say to myself in the mirror- "You are amazing and unique" which starts my day of on a positive note.

My advice would be if you get a free moment in the day, find something that would be funny to you and embrace in a happy surrounding. Whether it would be watching a film or a video, reading something or drawing something funny- Just do it and enjoy it. Having fun is now the present and future of my life and it will be yours as well.

"I live a happy life and future. I allow myself to embrace in fun and positivity as my life deserves the best"

If you require any more information on daily affirmations or personal help, please visit Growing Happily's website:

www.growinghappily.com

So from here I shall say my personal message to you all which is I hope you have enjoyed this helpful book and I trust and believe that each and every one of you who have read the book are going to be successful and live a happy and well deserved life.

Best Regards, Paul Errands x (Aged 17)

SD - #0032 - 070726 - C0 - 210/148/2 - PB - 9781780352824 - Gloss Lamination